Wonders of America

The Rocky Mountains

For the Hendrick family—M. D. B.

For Sophia, Leonardo, Tessa,
and Anna—J. G. W.

ALADDIN PAPERBACKS
An imprint of Simon & Schuster Children's Publishing Division
1230 Avenue of the Americas, New York, NY 10020
Text copyright © 2006 by Marion Dane Bauer
Illustrations copyright © 2006 by John Wallace
READY-TO-READ is a registered trademark of Simon & Schuster, Inc.
ALADDIN PAPERBACKS and colophon are trademarks of
Simon & Schuster, Inc.
Designed by Christopher Grassi
The text of this book was set in Century Old Style.
Manufactured in the United States of America
First Aladdin Paperbacks edition October 2006
2 4 6 8 10 9 7 5 3 1
Library of Congress Cataloging-in-Publication Data
Bauer, Marion Dane.
The Rocky Mountains / by Marion Dane Bauer ;
illustrated by John Wallace.
p. cm.—(Wonders of America)
ISBN-13: 978-0-689-86948-8 (pbk)
ISBN-10: 0-689-86948-7 (pbk)
ISBN-13: 978-0-689-86949-5 (library)
ISBN-10: 0-689-86949-5 (library)
1. Rocky Mountains—Description and travel—Juvenile literature.
2. Natural history—Rocky Mountains—Juvenile literature.
I. Wallace, John, 1966– ill. II. Title. III. Series: Bauer, Marion Dane.
Wonders of America.
F721.B28 2006
917.804—dc22
2005028026

Wonders of America

The Rocky Mountains

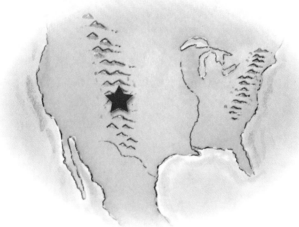

By **Marion Dane Bauer**

Illustrated by **John Wallace**

Ready-to-Read
ALADDIN
New York London Toronto Sydney

The Rocky Mountains
form the backbone
of North America.
That backbone is more than
3,000 miles long.

The Rockies take
their name from
their rocky peaks.

The Rocky Mountains form
North America's
Continental Divide.

They divide the rivers
that flow
to the Atlantic Ocean
from those that flow
to the Pacific Ocean.

Coyotes

and wolves,

bison

and elk live in
the Rocky Mountains.

Mountain lions live there,

and grizzly bears do too.

So do Rocky Mountain goats

and bighorn sheep.

Ptarmigans (tar-mi-guns),
birds with feathers
on their feet,
live in the cold,
rocky peaks.

People live in
the Rockies too.
People have lived there
for the last 11,000 years.

When the first settlers
arrived from Europe,
Shoshone lived in Idaho,

Blackfeet in Montana,

and Utes in Colorado.

Now many different
people live in the
Rockies.

Others come to visit
the mountains from
all over the world.

Some come to hike

and some to ski.

Some come to climb
the mountains.

Some come just to be

part of the quiet beauty.

We are very lucky
that the Rocky Mountains
are here today.

Our country has
a beautiful backbone!

Interesting Facts about the Rocky Mountains

★ To be called a mountain, land must rise to 1,000 feet or more. Many of the Rocky Mountains are more than 14,000 feet tall. In Colorado alone more than 50 peaks are over 14,000 feet.

★ The Rocky Mountains formed in different ways. The earth wrinkled to make some of them. Some were made because the earth cracked. Then pressure pushed one side of the crack up. Volcanoes made some of the Rocky Mountains. They poured out hot liquid that cooled into rock. All this happened long, long ago.

★ Over a long, long time mountains can be worn down by wind and dust. They can also be worn down by sliding snow and ice. Rain wears a mountain down too.

★ The Rockies get very little rain. They do get snow, though. Most of the water that feeds the mountains and the land around them comes from melted snow.

★ Lewis and Clark were among the first white explorers to cross the Rockies. When they got to the top of the first pass, they expected to be able to ride a river down the other side all the way to the Pacific Ocean. What they saw from that pass were many, many more mountains.